IMAGES

of America

TWIN FALLS

Ezra Meeker was an Oregon Trail pioneer who traversed the Idaho desert in 1852, ultimately settling in Washington state. In 1906, at the age of 76, he retraced the trail in an effort to preserve the story of the Western migration and to encourage communities to place markers along the route. He took his entourage across America and met Pres. Theodore Roosevelt, from whom he solicited support. Meeker wrote that "there is nothing like an ox-team journey, I maintain, to make a person realize this country, realize its size, the number of its people and the variety of conditions in which they live and of occupations by which they live." In this photograph, he is visiting Twin Falls in 1906. (Courtesy Bill Nichols.)

ON THE COVER: Clarence Bisbee (1876–1954) documented the celebration of the Fourth of July in 1912 in Twin Falls. This view shows the spectators watching the parade at the corner of Main Avenue and Shoshone Street, the center of the original town site and the city's downtown. At this time, Twin Falls was not even a decade old but had the modern conveniences and building types that could be found in much older communities. (Courtesy Bill Nichols.)

IMAGES
of America

TWIN FALLS

Elizabeth Egleston Giraud

ARCADIA
PUBLISHING

Published by Arcadia Publishing
Charleston, South Carolina

Library of Congress Control Number: 2009937669

For all general information contact Arcadia Publishing at:
Telephone 843-853-2070
Fax 843-853-0044
E-mail sales@arcadiapublishing.com
For customer service and orders:
Toll-Free 1-888-313-2665

Visit us on the Internet at www.arcadiapublishing.com

To my parents, Marvin and Helen Egleston, who let me wander but always welcomed me home; to my brother, Paul Egleston, who inspires me to follow my dreams; and to my husband, Richard Giraud, a true son of southern Idaho

CONTENTS

Acknowledgments   6

Introduction   7

1.   Life before Irrigation   9

2.   Ira Burton Perrine   23

3.   Reclamation Transforms the Desert   33

4.   Promoting the Tract   53

5.   The Business of Agriculture   61

6.   Building Communities   79

7.   Establishing Institutions   101

8.   The Comfort of Home   119

ACKNOWLEDGMENTS

Special thanks go to Bill Nichols of Blip Printing, Twin Falls, Idaho, for the use of Clarence Bisbee's photographs. This book would not be possible without his generosity and also the services of his staff, especially Lorin Robbins. Unless otherwise noted, all photographs are those of Clarence Bisbee provided by Bill Nichols.

Photographs from Brigham Young University (BYU), Provo, Utah, are courtesy of the L. Tom Perry Special Collection, Harold B. Lee Library, C. R. Savage Collection. Photographs from the Denver Public Library (DPL) are from the Western History Collection. Photographs from the Historic American Engineering Record (HAER) are courtesy of the National Park Service (NPS), Library of Congress (LOC.) Other collections from which photographs were obtained include the Shipler Collection, Utah State Historical Society (USHS); the Church of Jesus Christ of Latter-day Saints (LDS) Church History Library; the Idaho State Historical Society (ISHS); the William Henry Jackson Collection, Colorado Historical Society (CHS); the Twin Falls Public Library, the Twin Falls County Historical Museum (TFCHM); and the Northeastern Nevada Museum.

I also appreciate the help of Howard Moon, longtime historian of the Twin Falls region and especially of the Twin Falls Land and Water Company. Joe Webster of the Twin Falls Canal Company (TFCC) spent hours explaining the layout of the dam and canal system, which was very helpful. Former colleagues Judy Austin and Ann Swanson provided support and encouragement, and historic preservation friends in Twin Falls Shauna Robinson and Paul Smith provided valuable advice and materials. My timely encounters with Dan Everhart of the Idaho Transportation Department, Toni Mendive of the Northeastern Nevada Museum, and Mychel Matthews of the Twin Falls County Historical Museum were especially fruitful. I am also indebted to the many historians who have chronicled Twin Falls's history, including Jim Gentry, Virginia Ricketts, Mark Fiege, Hugh Lovin, and Leonard Arrington.

INTRODUCTION

This book tells the story of Twin Falls, Idaho, whose existence is owed to a vast irrigation system constructed during the first decade of the 20th century. The various reclamation projects were known as "tracts," in which federal land was segregated and made available for cultivation. Reclamation led to agricultural development and the establishment of communities that make up the economic network of the region.

Twin Falls is associated with the South Side Irrigation Tract. Milner Dam and its related canal system were constructed as part of the South Side tract and brought water to over 240,000 acres on the south side of the river once the project opened in 1905. Other reclamation tracts in the area opened soon after, including the Salmon River, North Side, and Minidoka tracts. Irrigation transformed a sagebrush desert into a rich agricultural area, and within only a few years, the last part of Idaho to be settled could offer the same amenities found anywhere.

The South Side project was made possible by the Carey Act of 1894 and is considered its most successful example. Named for Wyoming senator Joseph Carey, the federal legislation provided a mechanism to combine private investment, state oversight, and federal land for settlement. Many projects, including the Salmon River irrigation tract discussed in this book, did not fare as well due to overestimating the amount of water available and the financial problems of the investors.

The officials of the Twin Falls Land and Water Company, the corporation formed in 1900 to provide financial backing and leadership in building the system, experienced difficulties during the implementation of the project, but compared to many other Carey Act projects, the construction of the system progressed smoothly. The success of the project was the result of the volume of water available from the Snake River, the skill of engineers such as Walter Filer and Mark Murtaugh, and the connections of early investors Ira Perrine and Stanley Milner. These connections led to the capital investment of Frank Buhl, a wealthy businessman from Sharon, Pennsylvania. Ultimately it was his financial risk and management acumen that led to the fortunate outcome of the project.

The irrigation company officials promoted the project nationally and used the services of photographer Clarence Bisbee, whose photographs compose the bulk of this book. Bisbee came to Twin Falls early in 1906, and although he also had a studio business, he is best remembered for the events, people, and buildings he recorded regarding southern Idaho's development. Although he photographed subjects in neighboring towns, he did not go as far afield as some of his contemporaries, and his known work is limited to south-central Idaho. Sadly his success in recording the tract put him out of business. As the area grew, he had more competition, and the need for his photographs as a promotional tool diminished. Local accounts state that he died penniless in 1954.

Earlier photographers played an important role in recording the area in its pre-reclamation days. The development of the wet-plate collodion process allowed photographs to be reproduced and thus widely distributed in publications with national readership. After the Civil War, Congress invested

7

in explorations of the American West, with the intent of encouraging settlement and developing the region's natural resources. Photographers and artists accompanied these expeditionary parties to record the landscape, which were used to advance various political and economic agendas.

Timothy O'Sullivan, who accompanied Clarence King's U.S. Geological Exploration of the 40th Parallel and Capt. George Montague Wheeler's U.S. Geological Exploration West of the 100th Meridian, visited Shoshone Falls with both parties beginning in 1868 and took more pictures of it than any other site. He described the falls as "one of nature's greatest spectacles" and took special pains to visit Shoshone Falls in 1874 before leaving the West for good.

Although settlement in the Twin Falls area was sparse prior to reclamation, people were settling the region. As local historian Virginia Ricketts stated, mining was the agent for change. When Idaho's gold rush started in 1863, the demand for access to the mining districts led to the establishment of a home station at Rock Creek as a small oasis south of present-day Hansen. Rock Creek evolved into a small community that served travelers, miners, and ranchers for 20 years. Other activity in the area included gold placer mining at the bottom of the Snake River canyon, the cattle ranch of Arthur D. Norton and M. G. Robinson at Cottonwood Creek, and Toano Road freighting in the western part of the county.

The arrival of the railroad in Shoshone in 1883 led to further development. New arrivals such as Charles Walgamott, who came to the area as a young man in 1875, saw the potential of tourism to Shoshone Falls. A year later, Hermann Stricker, a German immigrant, settled in Rock Creek. After purchasing the Rock Creek store with John Botzet, he expanded his base, digging an irrigation ditch and homesteading additional land until his family holdings totaled 960 acres.

The infrastructure seems primitive by today's standards, but the availability of rail transportation and the expansion of the economic base led the pre-reclamation settlers to view Shoshone Falls as a potential tourism site. Ira Perrine, who developed his Blue Lakes farm at the bottom of the canyon, aggressively pursued many schemes to draw tourists to the falls. He, along with other area settlers, began envisioning irrigation as a means to develop the region.

The subject matter of this book is limited to the sites and events of Twin Falls County. Thus while the opening of nearby irrigation tracts such as the North Side and Minidoka impacted Twin Falls, the text and photographs in the book do not address these projects. The Salmon River tract, however, is included because it is located in Twin Falls County. For both practical and philosophical reasons, this book emphasizes the years from the opening of the irrigation tract through the 1910s. The practical reasons are that Bisbee took his best photographs during this period, and the book would be too voluminous to include the history of the county after the 1910s. The philosophical reason is that the optimism of the people and the wonder of the desert's transformation are best represented during these years.

One

LIFE BEFORE IRRIGATION

The Snake River plain may have been inhospitable to permanent white settlement before irrigation, but it was a crossroads for a variety of cultures with different intentions. For Native Americans, the environs of the Snake River provided shelter, food sources, and plentiful game. For immigrants, the region was a desolate test of endurance. As the area slowly developed, visitors saw potential to develop the area's resources for economic gain.

The small community of Rock Creek was the first permanent settlement in the area south of the Snake River. Rock Creek had water and rich grasslands and in 1864 became a home station for stage routes traveling between Kelton, Utah, and the northwest where travelers could rest and water their horses. Eventually the community included a store, post office, saloon, and was an important center for the handful of settlers who ranched and mined in the area prior to reclamation.

After the Civil War, Americans had more exposure to the western landscape through the availability of photographs taken on government-sponsored expeditions. Shoshone Falls was irresistible to photographer Timothy O'Sullivan, who accompanied both Clarence King and Lt. George Montague Wheeler on their federally sponsored journeys through the West. William Henry Jackson, who documented Ferdinand Hayden's exploration of Yellowstone, also photographed the falls. Salt Lake photographer Charles Savage not only visited the area prior to development but later documented the progress of the construction of Milner Dam.

Activity picked up in the 1870s. Prospectors discovered gold below Shoshone Falls, and sporadic mining along the bottom of the Snake River canyon continued for years. The completion of the transcontinental railroad in 1869 allowed freight activity between the rail terminus of Toano, Nevada, and the Wood River mining districts of Bellevue, Hailey, and Ketchum.

Mining enterprisers familiar with the Wood River activity saw the possibility of opening Shoshone Falls to tourism. Once rail transportation was available at Shoshone in 1883, visitors could take a stage to view the falls. In 1884, local pioneer Charles Walgamott obtained a license to operate a ferry at Shoshone Falls, and he and his wife opened a tent hotel on the north side of the canyon. By that time, Ira Burton Perrine, a pivotal figure in the history of southern Idaho, had arrived at Blue Lakes at the bottom of the Snake River Canyon.

MAGNITUDE
BISBEE 551

Shoshone Falls is the biggest drop in the Snake River as it winds its way from its headwaters in northwestern Wyoming and empties into the Columbia. Along the way, the river makes a wide arc across southern Idaho. Volcanic activity formed the geologic foundation of the land in south-central Idaho and resulted in lava flows, aquifers, and springs. For the farmers that later cultivated the area, the most important legacy of the ancient geologic activity was soil that was rich and fertile, once water reached it.

About 17,000 years ago, the Bonneville flood flowed through southern Idaho, carving the Snake River Canyon. For a great part of southern Idaho, the water simply covered hundreds of square miles, but near present-day Murtaugh, the water flow constricted, eroding downward at a rapid flow rate of about 15 million cubic feet per second. This photograph is of Pillar Falls, about 2 miles downstream of Shoshone Falls, which is evident in the background.

West of Shoshone Falls, springs from an aquifer discharge from the canyon walls. For thousands of years, the river and the springs provided a habitat supplying a bountiful food source for Native Americans, and the walls of the canyon provided shelter. In modern times, the warmer temperature of the springs has allowed an aquaculture industry to flourish in south-central Idaho.

Charles Roscoe (C. R.) Savage gazes out the window of his Salt Lake City home during the holidays. Savage, born in England, set up a photography studio upon arriving in Salt Lake in 1860. He photographed the West extensively, including Shoshone Falls, and was one of the photographers to record the joining of the transcontinental railroad in 1869. He was also the official photographer of the Milner Dam construction. Savage died in 1909 in Salt Lake City. (Courtesy BYU, MSS P 24 Item 807.)

GREAT SHOSHONE FALLS, SNAKE RIVER, IDAHO. O.SL.UEY, C.R.SAVAGE, SALT LAKE.

Historians date Savage's expansive photograph of Shoshone Falls to the late 1860s. With a large family to support, Savage did not have the freedom to participate in government surveys as did his contemporaries William Henry Jackson and Timothy O'Sullivan. He captured, however, many of the same images of the West's natural wonders through his association with railroads who used his photographs for promotional purposes. (Courtesy BYU, MSS P 24 Item 561.)

C. R. Savage took this stereographic photograph of Twin Falls, upstream from Shoshone Falls, about 1870. Developed in 1840, stereographs were a popular medium, allowing Americans to see images of far-flung places in the world in a three-dimensional format. (Courtesy BYU, MSS P 24 Item 68.)

William Henry Jackson was one of many artists and photographers drawn to Shoshone Falls and its environment. Jackson was trained as an artist but turned to photography after the Civil War. Much of his work was used for promotional purposes, first by the Union Pacific Railroad and later by Ferdinand Hayden. Jackson probably took this photograph of Twin Falls during one of his many trips West in the 1880s. (Courtesy CHS, Scan No. 20101090.)

Between 1868 and 1874, photographer Timothy O'Sullivan worked for Clarence King and George Montague Wheeler, who each led notable western expeditions after the Civil War. O'Sullivan visited Shoshone Falls at least twice, in 1868 and in 1874, and printed thousands of Western scenes. He died in Washington, D.C., in 1882. This O'Sullivan photograph shows members of King's party working at the top of the falls. (Courtesy DPL, No. Z-2678.)

O'Sullivan made more photographs of Shoshone Falls than of any other Western site. Whereas his boss, Clarence King, was repelled by the falls and found them threatening and unnerving, their fury entranced O'Sullivan. At the conclusion of his field season in 1874 photographing scenes of the Southwest, he traveled to Shoshone Falls by stagecoach on his own for what would be his last look at the falls. (Courtesy DPL, No. Z-2705.)

Two unidentified men stand to the right of artist Thomas Moran, who accompanied Ferdinand Hayden's survey of Yellowstone. Hayden used the skills of both Moran and photographer William Henry Jackson to convey the surreal features of Yellowstone to Congress, who established Yellowstone as the first national park. This photograph shows some of the unwieldy equipment photographers used to document places like Shoshone Falls. (Courtesy DPL, No. Z-6627.)

This photograph, taken by Jackson, shows a different perspective of the Snake River canyon. Jackson was trained as an artist but turned to photography after the Civil War. As a photographer, he worked in many camera formats and plate sizes and succinctly described the complex photographic process as "prepare, expose, develop, fix, wash, and dry." He died in 1942 at the age of 99. (Courtesy CHS, Scan No. 20101091.)

17

For 20 years, the small community of Rock Creek served travelers transporting freight between Utah and the Northwest. Stagecoach "king" Ben Holladay established Rock Creek as a home station in 1864, providing lodging and food for stage passengers and facilities for animals. James Bascom and John Corder opened a store in this log structure (above) in 1865 as part of the Rock Creek settlement, selling supplies to miners, ranchers, and Oregon Trail emigrants. (Courtesy author.)

Herman Stricker, a German immigrant, purchased the store in 1876. The purchase included the log store, a stable, livery, and the log dwelling seen in the photograph above. This house was the first home of Herman and Lucy Stricker, who were married in 1882. (Courtesy ISHS, 80-13.23.)

After the Strickers lost their first home in a fire in 1907, they constructed the Victorian house seen in this photograph. Today a small collection of buildings and sites associated with Rock Creek and the Stricker home site are owned by the Idaho State Historical Society. (Courtesy ISHS, 80-13.17.)

Toano was a railroad terminus about 34 miles east of
Wells, Nevada, that connected southwest Idaho with the
Central Pacific Railroad. During the 1870s, passengers
could take the train to Toano and hire a freighter to
cross the Snake River plain to reach points north.
Toano Road freighters presented serious competition to
operators from Kelton, Utah, but by 1883, rail service
through southern Idaho ended the need for both Toano
and Kelton freight lines. (Courtesy Shauna Robinson.)

A mule team and wagons hauled passengers from Toano, Nevada, north to the Snake River, across
what is now the western part of Twin Falls County. Once they reached the river, travelers could take
established routes to Idaho's gold mining districts. (Courtesy Northeastern Nevada Museum.)

Completed in 1886, the Shoshone Falls Hotel was located just upstream from the falls themselves. The hotel was part of an effort by mining investors to improve the infrastructure for a growing tourism industry, including the installation of a ferry supported by a cable and the construction of a decent road from the town of Shoshone to the falls. The hotel burned down in 1915.

This photograph, attributed to William Henry Jackson, shows a ferry crossing above Shoshone Falls. Charles Walgamott, a pre-reclamation settler of the area, received a county license to operate the ferry in 1884. The ferry ceased transporting customers in 1940, thirteen years after the Twin Falls-Jerome Bridge opened. The prospect of the boat breaking loose and plummeting over the falls probably inspired trepidation, but the ferry had a good safety record. (Courtesy CHS, Scan No. 20102487.)

Two stagecoach drivers discovered gold near Shoshone Falls in 1869, leading to placer mining on the river. Although prospecting continued in the vicinity of Twin Falls for decades, a feasible recovery system was unavailable, and mining activity was intermittent. The photograph shows a waterwheel near Milner that supplied water to a flume to extract fine gold. (Courtesy ISHS, 81-41.1/a.)

Two

IRA BURTON PERRINE

Ira Burton Perrine is generally credited as the visionary who transformed south-central Idaho from sagebrush into farmland through irrigation, although revisionist historians have questioned this assumption. No one can deny, however, that he was a prodigious worker with a strong entrepreneurial bent who worked tirelessly to advance his economic interests and that of the area. Born in Delaware, Indiana, in 1861, Perrine came to Idaho in 1884, acquired a herd of cows, and supplied the mining communities in the Wood River Valley with milk. Looking for a place to winter his cattle, Charles Walgamott, an early pioneer, suggested the beautiful and curious Blue Lakes at the bottom of the Snake River Canyon downstream of Shoshone Falls. Taken by Blue Lakes and enthralled by the area, Perrine spent the rest of life on his farm at the bottom of the canyon until he died in 1943.

A skilled orchardist, Perrine acquired and planted thousands of fruit trees within only a few years of living at Blue Lakes. He built a comfortable home and married Hortense McKay in 1892, a native of Fillmore, Utah, and the 17-year-old daughter of a Shoshone hotelier. He improved the trails up either side of the canyon walls and shipped and sold his produce to the new markets of southeastern Idaho and Montana. He contributed to development of the tourist industry in the area by building the Blue Lakes Hotel on his ranch and starting a ferry and stagecoach service. He had commercial ventures in Shoshone, the nearest established community to the falls prior to reclamation. Perrine pursued these endeavors for 20 years prior to the large-scale irrigation of the land above the canyon floor.

Other settlers were considering the potential of irrigation and hydroelectric power in the vicinity of Shoshone Falls at the end of the 19th century. While Perrine might not have had the influence on the opening of the South Side tract to the extent history has ascribed to him, he had several fortuitous connections that were instrumental in bringing the irrigation tract to fruition. Once the Milner Dam construction was completed, Perrine played a key role in the success of the Twin Falls town site and pursued many schemes to promote and develop southern Idaho.

I. B. Perrine arrived in Idaho as a young man in 1883 and supplied milk to the miners of the Wood River Valley. A skilled farmer, dairyman, and orchardist, Perrine also proved to be the consummate entrepreneur. He is best known for his role in reclamation in south-central Idaho, but he also contributed to building the financial, transportation, and utility infrastructure of the area. He died in 1943 at the age of 82. (Courtesy TFCHS.)

Located about 3 miles downstream from Shoshone Falls, the stillness and startling blue of the unusual pools contrast sharply with the dark basalt of the canyon walls. According to his autobiography, in 1884 pioneer Charles Walgamott directed Perrine to Blue Lakes as a good place to winter cattle "without constant attention." (Courtesy LDS Church History Library.)

Perrine's home in the canyon at the Blue Lakes Ranch was located on the north side of the canyon. Always attuned to money-making endeavors, Perrine opened the Blue Lakes Hotel in 1891 and hosted many illustrious and wealthy guests whose exposure to the area provided valuable contacts for future development. After Perrine's death in 1943, the ranch stayed in the family until 1964, when the land was converted into golf courses.

The boardwalk, poplar trees, and canyon promontory in this image provide an up-close glimpse of the environment of Perrine's ranch. The scale of the landscape depicts the width of the canyon floor and the interplay that occurred between man-made elements and natural surroundings. (Courtesy BYU, MSS P 24 Item 660.)

Perrine cultivated his Blue Lakes Ranch for 20 years prior to the development of large-scale reclamation in the region. His farm eventually encompassed 1,000 acres. Perrine's success convinced him that the soil was rich and agriculture could be a successful venture on the Snake River Plain if water could be made available. (Used by permission, USHS. All rights reserved.)

Harry Shipler, a Salt Lake City photographer, took a series of photographs of this group of people in early June 1912. He documented their travels through the countryside as they took in the sights of the canyon and falls and enjoyed Perrine's hospitality. In the photograph above, the visitors are gathered at Perrine's home at his Blue Lakes ranch. Below, they pose for Shipler at Perrine's "in-town" house, located at 110 Sixth Avenue N, Twin Falls. The home is no longer standing. (Both used by permission, USHS. All rights reserved.)

This photograph of a man picking dewberries is one of scores of Clarence Bisbee's photographs extolling the agricultural fertility of the Twin Falls region. Bisbee noted the age of the dewberry vines (one year) and the amount netted from the crop ($700). Dewberries are small, purplish berries similar to raspberries and blackberries.

Perrine's bridge across the Snake River at his ranch was one of several projects he undertook to ease travel to his ranch. Upon settling in the area in 1884, he began building roads to the rims of the canyon and later constructed this bridge.

Utah photographer C. R. Savage captured this young girl with peaches at Perrine's farm about 1890. Perrine had thousands of fruit trees at his Blue Lakes Ranch, and as settlement in southern Idaho took shape, his markets expanded. He sold fruit to the Albion State Normal School, for example, when it opened in 1893, and by 1896, he shipped fruit to Pocatello and Butte, Montana. He entered his fruit in many exhibitions in the United States and Europe. (Courtesy LDS Church History Library.)

Shoshone Falls promoters had discussed options to bring tourists to see the site as early as 1890, but it was not until Perrine instigated an electric railroad system between Twin Falls and Shoshone Falls in 1914 that it became a reality. He purchased storage-battery railroad cars from a company owned by Thomas Edison, but his electric transit system was soon supplanted by the automobile. The photograph above includes one of the electric railroad cars, which is in front of the building that housed the offices of the Shoshone Falls Power Company, another of Perrine's schemes. Below, businessmen in office attire ceremoniously complete the streetcar line.

Among the many functions Perrine played in building the new tract and city of Twin Falls was serving as the first president of the First National Bank. Perrine used the mortgages and contracts he accumulated by selling water rights to settlers of the tract as capital. Clarence Bisbee took this photograph of the bank within a few years of its construction in 1905. The building remains on the corner of Shoshone and Main Streets, but alterations to the building, probably dating to the 1960s, have caused the structure to lose all resemblance to its former self.

Stage transportation between Twin Falls and Jerome was another Perrine enterprise. In this photograph, the stage is loaded with men leaving from the Perrine Hotel, presumably for Jerome, a town site that opened on the North Side Tract in 1907. New communities associated with the other irrigation tracts opened in quick succession in south-central Idaho and expanded the economic base of Twin Falls.

Three

RECLAMATION
TRANSFORMS THE DESERT

The permanent settlement of Twin Falls County is the result of successful large-scale reclamation, made possible through the Carey Act of 1894. Known as the Twin Falls South Side tract, the reclamation project segregated over 240,000 acres of federal land with access to water from the Snake River.

Frank Riblett, a Rock Creek resident and surveyor, prepared plans for an irrigation system as early as 1881 but lacked the money to execute a reclamation project. Ira Perrine's association with Stanley Milner, the owner of extensive mining interests in Utah and Nevada, proved to be the critical connection in finding the necessary capital. With other investors, Perrine and Milner incorporated the Twin Falls Land and Water Company in 1900. When the company was forced to reorganize in 1902, Milner and his assistant, Walter Filer, convinced Pennsylvania industrialist Frank Buhl to back the project. It was Buhl's involvement that led to the successful resolution of the reorganization and, ultimately, the completion of the project.

The irrigation project consists of Milner Dam and a water delivery system of 1,100 miles of canals and laterals. Milner Dam was built at the Cedars on the Snake River, named for the cedars and scrub oak that covered two islands about 19 miles upstream of Shoshone Falls. Faris and Kesl, a Boise construction firm, began building the system in mid-March 1903 and finished two years later. The design of the dam was not complicated, as it basically involved building three cribs between the two islands, filling the cribs with dirt and rock fill, and then connecting the islands with the banks of the river.

Work on the canal system started the same time as the dam and resulted in a main canal, from which two others branched off: the High Line and the Low Line canals. In 1909, the Idaho State Land Board approved the irrigation company's request to accept the project and deem it complete and in working order. Upon state acceptance, the Twin Falls Canal Company was incorporated with the responsibility of maintaining the dam and canal system.

The outcome of the Twin Falls Salmon River tract, located immediately south of Twin Falls, was not as successful as the South Side tract. The tract opened to settlement in 1908 but was beset with problems. After years of legal disputes, subscribers took over the operation of the system and formed the Salmon River Canal Company.

The irrigation company's first task was constructing the bridge seen in this photograph. The bridge was located downstream from the Cedars, the eventual location of Milner Dam, and provided access between the construction site and the rail lines located on the north side of the Snake River. (Courtesy HAER, NPS, LOC, 27-TWIF.V.1-171.)

The man in this photograph is standing on the bank of the south island, after the bridge was built but prior to construction of the temporary power dam. A Crawford Placer mining wheel was located across the river. Clappine Rock is in the center of the photograph, named for the voyageur who perished in the Wilson Price Hunt party in 1811 as the explorers sought routes to the Pacific. (Courtesy HAER, NPS, LOC, 27-TWIF.V.1-175.)

Photographs of the Riverside Hotel are reminders that Milner was once a thriving town with a population of about 1,500. The hotel was constructed in 1908 by the Kuhn brothers, who invested in other irrigation projects in the area. Demolished in 1923, for a few years it offered a nearby respite to guests from the Twin Falls area and those wishing to enjoy the view of the dam and the river.

Working conditions were bleak for those constructing Milner Dam. Laborers worked in all weather conditions with no shade, had only tents for shelter, and could afford few amenities, such as beds, baths, or meals in Rock Creek or the Stricker Ranch. With the use of explosives, the work was often dangerous. Building the dam and related canal system required about 500 men and 400 teams of horses. (Courtesy Joe Webster, TFCC.)

The electricity produced by an on-site temporary hydroelectric power dam greatly facilitated the construction of the project. After the narrow-gauge boxcars were filled with rocks and earth, they were transported to the cranes, which then hoisted the cars, moved the fill above the desired place, and dumped the fill. The railroad, the cranes, and other construction equipment operated via the electric power produced by the power dam. (Courtesy HAER, NPS, LOC, 27-TWIF.V.1-165.)

"Taylor work" is illustrated in this photograph. The phrase refers to the effort to drill the upper layer of rock on the north side of the river in order to carve a channel for what became the North Side Canal. The excavated rock was then taken to the north dam site and dropped into the river to construct the dam.

Workers constructed a tunnel in the south island to divert water from the channel, where the main flow of the river occurred, in order to facilitate construction of the north dam. The photograph above shows the tunnel construction in progress. The photograph below illustrates the concreted approach to the tunnels from the downstream side. (Both courtesy HAER, NPS, LOC; above, 27-.TWIF.V.1-168; below, 27-.TWIF.V.1-182.)

The large dredge was used to build the lower end of the Main Canal, originally referred to as the South Side Canal. In the photograph above, the dredge is near Murtaugh Lake. (Courtesy Joe Webster, TFCC).

Looking south from behind the old North Side Canal spill gates, this photograph provides an expansive view of the Milner Dam spill gates and "Irrigation Falls," a nickname provided by C.R. Savage, the official photographer of the construction of the dam.

Instead of using a siphon, subcontractors constructed this 400-foot-long timber flume across Cottonwood Creek, a branch of Rock Creek, to carry the water of the High Line Canal. (Courtesy HAER, NPS, LOC, 27-TWIF.V.1-177; Photograph by Clarence Bisbee, September 1912.)

To accommodate the drop of Rock Creek Canyon, south of Kimberly, the company used this steel pipe to transport the water of the Low Line Canal across the canyon. The siphon was manufactured in Pennsylvania, shipped to Idaho with an installment crew, and took four months to assemble. In this photograph, James Schuyler is on the left, Filer is the middle figure standing, Buhl is on the right, and Peter Kimberly is seated. (Courtesy HAER, NPS, LOC, 27-TWIF.V.1-87; Photograph by C. R. Savage, date unknown.)

Although initially Filer and the other engineers believed one canal could deliver water to the entire South Side tract, they realized the difficult topography required two canals. The Main Canal splits into the Low and High Line canals at the Forks, about 10 miles downstream from Murtaugh Lake. The Low Line Canal drops 90 feet at the Forks and winds through the tract for about 35 miles. The High Line Canal is longer and is south of the Low Line Canal. It continues west for about 47 miles before emptying into Deep Creek.

Walter Filer, a civil engineer, was the general manager of the project. He carried the responsibility for much of the design work and the construction oversight. Filer worked for Stanley Milner in Salt Lake. It was through Filer that engineers Mark Murtaugh, a college classmate, and Paul Bickel, a former engineering colleague, came to the project. Filer's most important connection, however, was industrialist and financier Frank Buhl of Sharon, Pennsylvania, where Filer had grown up. (Courtesy TFCHM.)

The ditches being dug in this photograph may not be related to the South Side tract, but the photograph illustrates how dirty, difficult, and cumbersome creating and maintaining irrigation systems could be. (Courtesy Joe Webster, TFCC.)

Island, below spillway

Tunnel outlet

The impounded water of the Snake River poured over the spillway of the dam when the project opened in 1905, and the sight of the manmade waterfall presented its own dramatic beauty. Buildings in Milner can be seen in the background.

Stanley Milner came to the project through his association with Perrine, whom he knew from studying mining sites on the Snake River. A native of Wisconsin, he was an investor in mining companies in Utah and Nevada. Milner's involvement in the project was limited to financial backing and management. He died in 1906, just after the opening of the Buhl town site. (Courtesy TFCHM.)

The vital backer of the project, Frank Buhl was a wealthy businessman from Sharon, Pennsylvania. After two of the original investors dropped out in 1902, it was not until Walter Filer and Witcher Jones, a Salt Lake mining acquaintance, interested Buhl that viable financing became available. They encouraged Buhl to visit the proposed tract, which he did with his wife, Julia, in November 1902. Buhl not only provided his own capital but interested other wealthy Eastern investors as well. (Courtesy TFCHM.)

A large crowd gathered on top of the deck of Milner Dam for the official closing of the tunnel gates on March 1, 1905. As the gates closed, the water began to back up toward the opening of the South Side or Main Canal. Within a few hours, the water reached the gates of the canal and the river flowed over the spillway of the dam.

This panoramic scene provides a view of many of the landmarks associated with both the South Side and North Side irrigation projects: Milner Dam, the Riverside Hotel, the Martin B. DeLong residence, the town of Milner, and the North Side Canal. The North Side irrigation system was

undertaken by the Kuhn brothers of Pittsburgh, incorporated as the Twin Falls North Side Land and Water Company in 1907. (Courtesy Joe Webster, TFCC.)

Constructed during 1909 and 1910, the Salmon Falls Dam is a gravity-fed arch dam, visually notable for its graceful appearance. The dam cost $3.6 million to construct and measures 223.5 feet high. The dam was the centerpiece of the Twin Falls Salmon River tract, which ultimately delivered less than a quarter of the water promised to settlers.

The incorporation of a roadway on the top of the dam was an unusual but functional feature, as it could accommodate people, vehicles, and livestock. Although historically the Salmon irrigation project failed to meet the expectations of settlers and investors, today the Salmon River Canal Company supplies water to the users of 35,000 acres and services several hundred miles of canals and laterals.

Andrew J. Wiley designed the Salmon Falls Dam. A protégé of civil and mining engineer Arthur Foote, here he is pictured on the left in 1889 while in Foote's employ. Born in Delaware about 1863, Wiley came west as a young man and had a successful career both as an engineer and as a consultant to federal agencies on many of the West's most significant dams. Many accounts attribute the design of Milner Dam to both Filer and Wiley. (Courtesy ISHS, 69-25.3.)

Construction crews had to transport materials to the Salmon Falls Dam site with these "traction trains," three-wheeled steam engines with a wide center wheel for traction. In 1910, once the railroad advanced to Rogerson, 8 miles east of the dam, moving supplies became easier.

This photograph illustrates both the location of the dam in the Salmon River Canyon and the construction activity. Because the dam was remote, the contractor, F. C. Home, economized by using a large amount of basalt from the canyon walls. Basalt was quarried to be crushed, used for concrete, and cut into blocks, which were used within the forms to strengthen the walls of the dam.

People gather for the opening of the Hollister town site on October 2, 1909. Promotional literature promised trees, rail access to Twin Falls, and inexpensive electricity, but like the other town sites associated with the Salmon tract, Hollister's growth was tied to the success of the irrigation project and failed to fulfill the investors' expectations. The town was named after Harry L. Hollister, an investor in the Wood River mining district and hydroelectric power.

The first irrigation water arrived on the Salmon project on June 6, 1911, but within the first year, only 6,000 acres were in production, a fraction of the 70,000 acres entered in the first three days of the 1908 land draw. In an effort to bolster confidence, Clarence Bisbee's photograph portrayed the results of "the second year of cultivation" next to a silo in Hollister.

The buildings seen in this photograph of Hollister's first years were typical of those first constructed in any of the towns associated with southern-Idaho irrigation tracts. The buildings were frame, sheathed with clapboard siding, and often had a parapet or false front to make them look as impressive as possible. (Courtesy Twin Falls Public Library, GB-56.)

This commercial structure was one of Hollister's most imposing buildings and housed the Hollister Bank, a store, and the services of Dr. Parrott, an optometrist. Its appearance of stability gave the impression that Hollister would soon be a thriving trading center for the new tract, and indeed Hollister grew quickly during its first years but could not sustain its early momentum. (Courtesy Twin Falls Public Library, GB12.)

Located 4 miles from Hollister, this simple frame church was built in Amsterdam, one of the towns affiliated with the Salmon tract. Founded and platted in 1912, the town once had businesses, a school, a grain elevator, and this church, but the community eventually faded out. The church was later moved to Filer.

Residents of Hollister had high hopes for the success of their community when the school in this photograph was constructed in 1912. Hollister voters approved a $30,000 bond to construct this building, believing it would anchor their town as the trading center for the irrigation tract. Twin Falls architect Burton Morse designed it. The building's exterior conceals the unusual floor plan within: an open, octagonal hall in the center extending through all three stories.

Four

PROMOTING THE TRACT

The sluggish sales of the first opening, held on July 1, 1903, prompted the project's investors to commit more resources to marketing the farmland and town site. Officials hired a publicity expert, Mark Bennett, to promote the tract nationally, and the success of the second opening, held on October 4, 1904, was encouraging. The Twin Falls Investment Company incorporated to conduct real estate transactions for the project and hired Robert McCollum as its secretary and sales manager. Working from a small frame shack at what is now Main Avenue South, he sold $3 million worth of property by July 1905, an indication that the investors' speculation was worthwhile.

Advertising the area's merits did not end in the first years of the tract's existence. Twin Falls's boosters were untiring in their efforts to promote the tract for years. The Twin Falls Commercial Club contracted with *Pacific Monthly* to run advertisements, and national publications such as *Harper's* and *New West* magazines featured articles about irrigated desert land. Miniature irrigation systems were constructed at expositions such as the Alaska-Yukon-Pacific Exhibit, held in 1909 in Seattle, and in the same year the *Chicago Tribune* held a "big land show," which included information about Twin Falls, to benefit the "landless people of the Middle West."

Clarence Bisbee's photographs, used extensively throughout this book, are an invaluable legacy of the tract's promotion. Bisbee arrived in Twin Falls on January 27, 1906, at the urging of his friend Charles Diehl, the founder of the *Twin Falls News*. Diehl knew Bisbee from their photography training in Illinois, and for a number of years, Bisbee's photographic business flourished. He and his wife, Jessie, recorded agricultural production, civic events, street scenes, people, and buildings, in addition to producing portraits of individuals and families. As the development of the area matured, however, demand for Bisbee's services diminished; civic leaders focused their efforts in attracting new industries rather than promotion. This, coupled with the economic downturn in the West in the 1920s and 1930s, caused the Bisbees to lose everything. Jessie recalled both happier times and regret when she wrote, "It has been a great game. A great guess and a great gamble this throwing our youth, our strength, our dreams, and our ideals into a new desert country. Once is enough, though!"

An Idaho Land Drawing. Twin Falls, Idaho

The crowds of people gathered for the land drawing in this photograph were most likely assembled for the opening of the Salmon River tract, which opened on June 1, 1908. By this time, the Twin Falls South Side project appeared to be successful enough to encourage financiers to pursue reclamation ventures in the vicinity of the South Side tract. The first land drawing, on July 1, 1903, for the South Side tract disappointed company officials, but interest grew as work on Milner Dam progressed. The second opening for the South Side tract, held on October 20, 1904, was encouraging, and the response indicated that the project would succeed. Whatever project the photograph is associate with, the image presents the interest of newcomers in owning reclaimed desert land. (Courtesy ISHS 78-32.2.)

Newspaper editor McCollum (seated) met Perrine in Shoshone shortly after Perrine arrived in Idaho and remained involved in the region's economic development for many years. As a publisher and editor, McCollum was a natural fit to become the secretary and general sales manager of the project's investment company. John Hayes (standing) was an assistant to engineer Paul Bickel, the chief engineer of the irrigation project, and surveyed most, if not all, of the town sites on the Twin Falls tract. (Courtesy Twin Falls Public Library, G196.)

Robert McCollum and his wife, Elizabeth, lived in this house on Shoshone Avenue, considered to be the first house in Twin Falls. Constructed in part to present Twin Falls as a community of stability and comfort, the home was the gathering place of the "Homeless Twenty," young, single, well-educated professional men who became business leaders in Twin Falls. The house remains, but alterations have changed its appearance.

Clarence Bisbee poses in front of a stack of glass negatives used to record the events and development of south-central Idaho as its history unfolded. After he died in 1954, his negatives were sold at an estate auction but ultimately found their way to the Twin Falls Public Library.

Jessie Bisbee arrived in Twin Falls in 1910, four years after Clarence moved to the area. Although she has received scant attention in historical reports, the little information that does exist indicates that she worked alongside her husband in the field and studio. Jessie recounted her first years in Twin Falls with her husband as happy and fulfilled but described the financial hardship they suffered in the 1920s and 1930s as harrowing. She died in 1936, leaving Clarence to fend for himself until his death in 1954.

Bisbee worked out of a variety of spaces, including a tent, before he and Jessie built their studio and home on Second Street and Second Avenue East in 1914. The incorporation of the words "Life and Art are One" expressed not only their personal philosophy but the broader, contemporary sentiment associated with the Arts and Crafts movement. Bisbee's business declined as the need to advertise the tract diminished and other photographers provided competition. Legal efforts to save their business and retain the studio failed, leaving Bisbee penniless when he died.

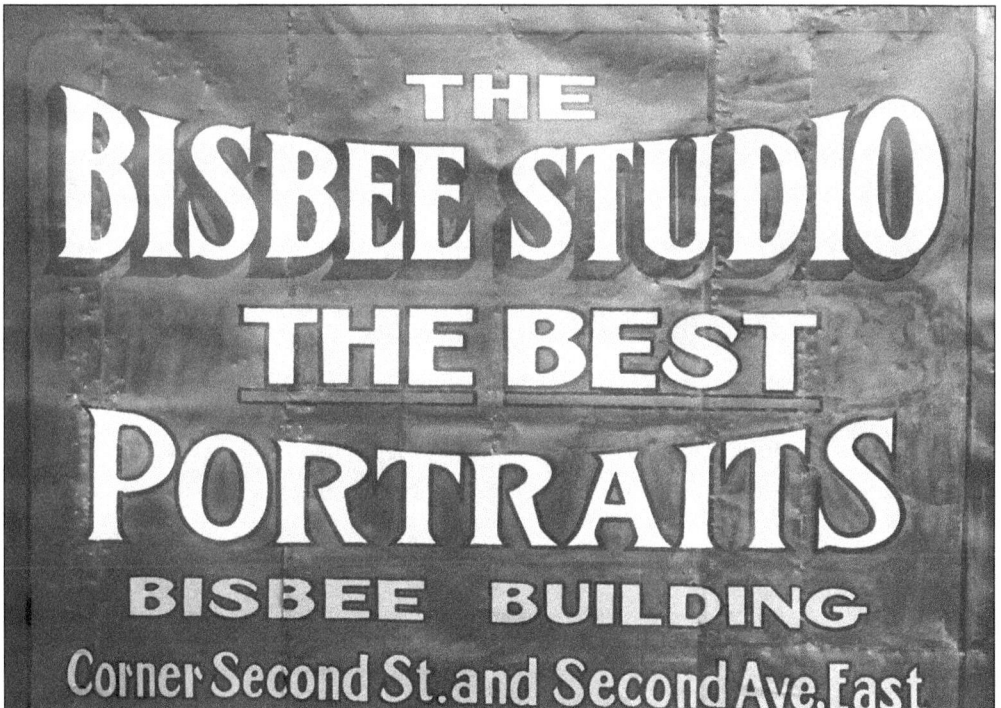

THE
BISBEE STUDIO
THE BEST
PORTRAITS
BISBEE BUILDING
Corner Second St. and Second Ave. East

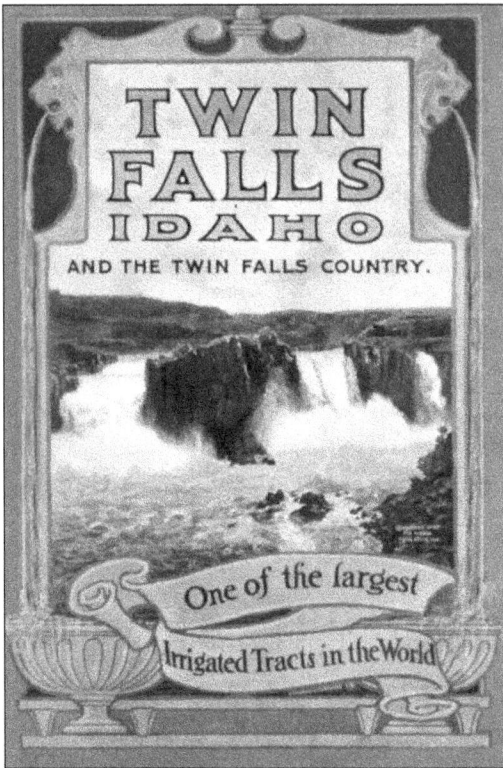

One of the largest Irrigated Tracts in the World

Organized in July 1905, the Twin Falls Commercial Club was the forerunner to the chamber of commerce, and no opportunity to promote or improve the area escaped their efforts. They lobbied government officials for infrastructure improvements, sought new industries, and supported civic institutions. The group produced promotional literature, the cover of which is seen to the left. In the photograph below, members gathered for their annual potato breakfast, at which Fillet of Salmon Tract, Rogerson Lamb Chops, and Murtaugh Mints were served.

First Annual Potato Breakfast
Commercial Club - 1-21-1911
Twin Falls, Idaho.

Bisbee Photo
337

In this Bisbee photograph of hunters entitled "30 Minutes Hunt," Bisbee indicated the ample game awaiting the visitor or resident in southern Idaho.

The fishermen in this photograph appear very nonchalant for having reeled in a 330-pound sturgeon. At the time this sturgeon was caught, they were more plentiful in the bottom of the Snake River below Shoshone Falls. Although dam construction and overfishing threatened the sturgeon, they continue to populate the Snake River near Hagerman.

The Perrine Hotel was a longtime landmark of downtown Twin Falls, until its demolition in 1968. It opened in December 1905 with modern amenities: running water, electricity, and a formal dining room. The imposing size and materials imparted an air of permanence to potential and new residents and provided comfortable surroundings in a harsh environment. The hotel was designed by architect J. Flood Walker, the architect of the popular Idaho Building at the Louisiana Purchase Exposition held in St. Louis in 1904.

Five

THE BUSINESS OF
AGRICULTURE

Farmers, of course, were the most important newcomers to the tract. They raised the crops, tended the livestock, and produced the harvest that created the agricultural economy of south-central Idaho. Farmers first faced the challenge of clearing their land of sagebrush and ridding their crops of rabbits and other pests. As Perrine had predicted, once water arrived the fertile soil was productive. Community boosters, aided by Clarence Bisbee's photographs, unceasingly proclaimed the plentiful agricultural yields made possible by irrigation.

The Twin Falls Land and Water Company established an experimental farm of 40 acres soon after the tract opened. The farm was located at the corner of Shoshone Street and Blue Lakes Boulevard and was managed by Alex McPherson, who served as a kind of company extension agent for the area. He published numerous articles and organized farmers' cooperatives. As early as 1907, he informed area farmers of the disease-resistant russet Burbank potatoes that are well suited to the climate and soil conditions of Idaho. By supporting farmers with its sponsorship of the experimental farm, the irrigation company helped ensure it would recoup its investment.

Like anywhere else, the marketing of agricultural goods produced by southern-Idaho farmers was not limited to local economic constraints or opportunities. Farmers were part of national and international economies, affected by events over which they had no control. Alfalfa seed production, for example, increased in Idaho during World War I, not only because of a greater wartime demand but also because the war cut off the imported supply from Central Asia.

The link to bigger markets was reflected in the early involvement of regional and national firms in warehouse districts of the new reclamation communities. The Twin Falls Milling and Elevator Company was a subsidiary of the Colorado Milling and Elevator Company that sold its flours nationally and, as early as 1913, exported to Asia. Local entrepreneurs who provided services or goods to farmers had great opportunities as well, and several firms dating to the first years of the tract successfully entered national markets. Blacksmiths, for example, diversified into manufacturing farm machinery and tools that were adapted for irrigated farming and later manufactured steel or opened plumbing and hardware businesses.

Clearing sagebrush was the first step in preparing the land for planting. Farmers used horse-drawn cutters to remove the sagebrush. A newspaper ad for the Hendricks Sagebrush Grubber claimed that, with a team of six horses, farmers could clear six or seven acres a day with the "knives placed so as to cut below the soil surface thus taking out the tougher sage brush roots and leaving the land ready for plowing."

As farmers cleared their land of sagebrush, rabbits turned to the crops and young trees for food. To combat them, organized parties of farmers drove them into enclosures and then clubbed or shot them. In the Christmas day edition of 1908, the *Twin Falls News* reported that 4,000 rabbits were killed two days before, "after which an excellent lunch was served." Within a few years, farmers turned to poison to eradicate the rabbits.

German immigrant Ernest Krengle established a blacksmith and hardware business in Twin Falls in 1907, working with his son, Charles, who managed the hardware section. After Ernest died of typhoid in 1912, Charles expanded the business, which eventually included an electrical department and a plumbing supply division. Charles invented, manufactured, and patented many agricultural tools, including the Twin Falls All-Steel Sage Brush Grubbers and Alfalfa Crowners.

Because wood frame was the dominant method of construction, lumber companies were some of the earliest businesses in what became the warehouse district of Twin Falls. In addition to the Twin Falls Lumber Company, the Nibley-Channel Company, based in Ogden, Utah, and the Adam-Pilgerrim Company provided building materials in the early years of the community, contributing to the rapid building campaigns in Twin Falls and nearby towns.

The success of Frederic Harder, a German immigrant, exemplifies the opportunities afforded by the new irrigation tracts. A baker by training, he opened Twin Falls's first bakery in 1905, and the availability of rail transportation meant that he could ship bread to Shoshone and the new towns of Rupert, Burley, and Gooding. In 1909, he and a partner, Charles Munson, established the Southern Idaho Wholesale Grocery Company, a wholesale produce and grocery concern. The products Harder and Munson sold illustrate the variety of products local farmers produced: potatoes, onions, beans, apples, berries, eggs, and honey. Harder and his wife, Caroline (known as Carrie), had their own farm on Blue Lakes Boulevard, seen in these photographs.

Agricultural associations and cooperatives enabled farmers to market their products more efficiently and hopefully more profitably. The warehouses, located south of downtown near rail access, provided as optimal conditions as possible to ensure that crops and produce did not spoil before reaching their markets.

Disk implements offered another option to breaking up sagebrush. They not only uprooted the sage but chopped the plant, its roots, and the obstinate soil below in a single pass. The discs also prepared the ground for planting.

Although crops such as wheat and alfalfa hay were not as labor intensive throughout the growing season as row crops (sugar beets and potatoes), harvesting grain required large crews to cut, gather, and thresh the grain. Family-run farms relied on neighbors to share and trade labor, while the owners of large, irrigated farms hired workers for wages. In this photograph, the men are stacking hay.

Alfalfa hay was useful in many ways to farmers: its cultivation enriched the soil, it provided feed to animals, and its seed could be sold for farmers in other regions to raise their own alfalfa crop. Because of its versatility, farmers of irrigated land allocated 36 percent of their acreage to alfalfa by 1910. Although the prices for the commodity fluctuated dramatically over time, shifting market forces presented an ongoing need for the crop.

After wheat was gathered and allowed to dry, the threshing process began. Just as families helped one another harvest the crops, farmers of small operations sometimes pooled their resources and shared the cost of machinery. The crews fed the sheaves into the machine, which loosened and separated the grain from the chaff, and the spewed-out grain was then bagged and taken to the grain elevator.

The market for alfalfa remained steady through the 1910s and even through the 1920s, when commodity prices steeply declined. Sheep men and cattle ranchers required alfalfa hay, as rangeland continually decreased due to overstocking and the expansion of irrigated farmland. Nationally farmers bought alfalfa seed in order to grow their own hay. After World War I, Americans consumed an increasing amount of dairy products, sustaining a demand for alfalfa hay as feed for dairy cows.

Early rail access and the rapid development of agricultural land attracted national processing companies, such as the Twin Falls Milling and Elevator Company (above), a subsidiary of a Colorado company with mills, elevators, and processing sites throughout the West. Between 1909 and 1916, the Twin Falls operation attained a storage capacity of 250,000 bushels of grain. The facility stored and processed a variety of agricultural products, including seeds and beans. It was best known for its flours, to which it attached regional identity with names such as Idahome, Twinida, and Shone-mist, as well as Duncan Hines, a cake flour later marketed by another company. The men in a warehouse doorway on the left appear to be associated with a merchant class, made possible by the local agricultural wholesale and processing activity.

Bisbee noted the warehouse in the photograph above as "the first seed warehouse." It also displays the use of "mill construction," referring to the structural system consisting of heavy timbers and thick plank floors initially developed for use in New England textile mills. Such construction impeded fire and allowed time to extinguish fires and salvage stored items. Attention to fireproofing warehouses helped owners avoid high insurance rates and assured sellers their stock would be safe until it went to market. The owners of the Isbell Seed Company took fire protection a step further by cladding the building with corrugated metal.

The Lincoln Produce and Refrigeration Company was founded in 1910. Before mechanized refrigeration was available, ice was crucial for preventing the spoilage of produce. Lincoln Produce manufactured ice, as opposed to cutting it from winter ponds. Local accounts from the time also praised the business for making good ice cream and butter.

The trucks seen in this photograph are associated with the Warberg family, who operated a transfer, storage, and coal company established by a Swedish immigrant, William Warberg. After moving to Twin Falls in 1905, Warberg started a hauling business with a team of horses, quickly expanding with additional teams and a Buick truck by 1913. Warberg's sons began similar concerns and gradually expanded to nationwide service through Allied Van Lines.

KUNZE CHEESE FACTORY
AR BUHL IDAHO
BISBEE 658

The Gustav Kunze dairy barn is one of several barns associated with dairymen from Tillamook, Oregon, who moved to the Buhl area about 1910. The inexpensive land and plentiful alfalfa attracted them, and when Kunze started a cheese factory in 1912, the dairymen had a convenient buyer for the milk their dairy cows produced. A German-Russian immigrant, Henry Schick, constructed the barns, which represent a hybrid of traditional building techniques and an awareness of progressive ideas espoused in agricultural literature.

Like potatoes, sugar beets were ideally suited to cultivation in the irrigated land of southern Idaho. The Twin Falls sugar factory was constructed east of the city in 1916, the year after Utah entrepreneurs David Eccles and Charles Nibley founded the company. Amalgamated Sugar Company contracted with local farmers to produce the beets and was an important source of both seasonal and permanent employment for area residents.

Obviously town residents did not cultivate crops on the extensive scale seen on irrigated farms, but they managed to make productive use of vacant city lots. Here children pose for Bisbee in a patch of giant onions.

Although it lacked the nitrogen-producing qualities of alfalfa, wheat was easy to grow, required less water than other crops, and needed minimal labor until harvesting. Wheat did well in soil that had not been nourished by alfalfa cultivation, and thus the first settlers on the tract produced it. This photograph is typical of many of Bisbee's photographs, in which the subjects advertise the ample production made possible through irrigation.

J. A. Waters arrived in the Twin Falls area in 1904 from Yakima, Washington, and established a successful dairy business. He raised alfalfa, corn, and fruit, and as the photograph of his home shows, he was also a skilled horticulturalist. A nurseryman, he supplied the trees that lined Blue Lakes Boulevard as well as the city park. Waters was active politically, serving in the state legislature and on the school board. His locust grove was the site of many community picnics, especially for pioneer associations.

Crates of apples are ready for shipping in this photograph, as one gentleman enjoys the content of the containers. Initially Twin Falls promoters envisioned the South Side tract as great orchard country, and indeed area farmers produced ample quantities of fruit, especially apples, peaches, and berries.

The owners of the High Line Seed Farm of Clover, south of Filer and Buhl, pose for Bisbee in front of the First National Bank in downtown Twin Falls. A banner attached to the wagon proclaims the yield per acre enjoyed by the owner, which Bisbee announced in his caption as $357 per acre, a "U.S. record as far as known."

Crops such as potatoes had a high labor demand, as they needed diligent tilling and watering during the growing season and concentrated labor at harvest. The legions of bags in the field behind the workers attest to the toil of harvesting spuds.

Potato diggers relieved some of the work of harvesting tubers by lifting the entire plant and separating the dirt and vines from the spuds. Once separated from the vine, crews placed the potatoes into buckets then used the sorter seen on the right to dump the spuds into burlap sacks.

TWIN FALLS, THE POTATO BELT.
BISBEE PHOTO—95.

This photograph portrays the "potato alley" found in many Idaho communities, where farmers and wholesalers lined up to deliver their spuds. Both corporate entities and farmer cooperatives managed warehouses where workers sorted, graded, and stored the tubers. After a federal grading standard was established in the 1910s, spuds meeting government standards could be used as collateral for federal loans. Grading potatoes, however, could be a source of friction between farmers and the wholesale buyers.

One Hill of Potatoes
Grown by J.R. Newton.
169
Bisbee Photo

Idaho farmers, wholesalers, and government officials worked hard to establish the Idaho spud as the best potato available, one that was standard in size, free from disease, and tasted the best, or as one historian described, "not just good spuds but outstanding, exceptional, wondrous ones." Associating Idaho potatoes as the "gold standard" for spuds enabled farmers and wholesalers to command a higher price. Bisbee intended to use this photograph to extol the agricultural fertility of the Twin Falls area, but the image of the attractive young woman also connotes the wholesomeness of what became the state's most celebrated product.

Six

BUILDING COMMUNITIES

Paul Bickel, the chief engineer of the Twin Falls Land and Water Company, considered several sites for the primary town of the irrigation tract. He and his assistant, John Hayes, who surveyed the section that became the town site, recognized its advantages. The location would accommodate a railroad grade; it was a school section, so that the land could be purchased outright without having to fulfill homesteading requirements; and Hayes was particularly taken with the possibility of Rock Creek Canyon serving as a scenic amenity to attract development. Between May and December 1904, Bickel submitted four plats that encompassed a square mile divided into 164 blocks.

The city of Twin Falls grew quickly. By the end of 1904, the town had 75 buildings; by 1906, it had a population of 3,000, a sewer system, water works, electric lights, telephones, and 400 buildings. Early access to rail transportation, available in August 1905, provided a critical transportation link with the rest of the state and the country. Nearby towns on the tract grew as well. The communities of Buhl, Filer, Murtaugh, Hansen, and Kimberly had schools, churches, and commercial districts, although on a smaller scale than Twin Falls. The establishment of other town sites on the tract and the opening of nearby irrigation tracts did not supplant Twin Falls's role as the economic center of south-central Idaho but instead reinforced it.

Expressing confidence in the future of the town, business owners used sturdy building materials, such as pressed concrete block, fired brick, and roughly cut basalt. During the years between 1910 and 1921, Twin Falls residents saw the construction of its most stylish buildings, generally associated with banks, fraternal organizations, and automobile dealerships. The opening of irrigated lands in south-central Idaho provided new opportunities for Idaho's small but accomplished architectural community. Burton Morse, Edward Gates, and B. Morgan Nisbett all lived in Twin Falls, designing buildings not only in Twin Falls but throughout southern Idaho. Boise firms such as Wayland and Fennell found commissions in Twin Falls, as did architects such as C. Harvey Smith of Spokane, who designed the county courthouse and the Twin Falls Bank and Trust, although Smith returned to Spokane after living in Twin Falls only a short time.

The arrival of the Oregon Short Line (OSL) Railroad early in Twin Falls's development was critical to the success of the tract. Unlike communities such as Shoshone and Pocatello, the railroad reached Twin Falls in response to the founding of the town rather than the town being established because a rail line was available. The OSL, a subsidiary corporation of the Union Pacific system, reached Twin Falls early in August 1905, branching off from the main line at Minidoka, north of the Snake River. The location of the depot parallel to Rock Creek Canyon, south of what would become downtown, meant that the surrounding land would be used for warehouse and industrial purposes, while residential neighborhoods would grow up around the park. (Above, courtesy ISHS, 80-90.11.)

Vacant lots and open ditches are all evident in the 1906 photograph of Twin Falls (above), indicating that the city was only recently settled. Within a decade, however, Twin Falls boasted fine business blocks of two- or three-story buildings. Wayland and Fennell, a Boise firm, designed the Baugh building on the left (below). Its construction on the corner of Shoshone and Main Streets, along with the Perrine Hotel and two banks on the other corners, created a formal focal point for the downtown.

The Twin Falls Bank and Trust was established on June 1, 1905, in the frame structure seen in the photograph on the left and was initially known as "McCornick's Bank," after its founder, William McCornick. A native of Canada, McCornick was a successful, self-made businessman who sought his fortune in the American West, eventually settling in Salt Lake City where he invested in mining, banking, and utility ventures. In 1909, he hired architect C. Harvey Smith to design the neoclassical style building seen below. Smith was also the architect of the county courthouse.

The Snake River and Shoshone Falls not only inspired dreams of reclaiming the surrounding arid land for cultivation but also of developing hydroelectric power. In 1900, Perrine interested a mining associate, Harry Hollister, in investing in a power plant facility and subsequently filed a claim for 3,000 cubic feet per second of water from each side of the Snake River. Originally intended for irrigation purposes, these water claims also eventually served the future power plant. Construction of the hydroelectric power plant took six years and was executed intermittently, but in August 1907, water was turned into the system for the first time, producing 500 kilowatts of power. William Kuhn, who had taken over the project in 1907, went bankrupt in 1913, and by 1916, the project was under the aegis of the Idaho Power Company.

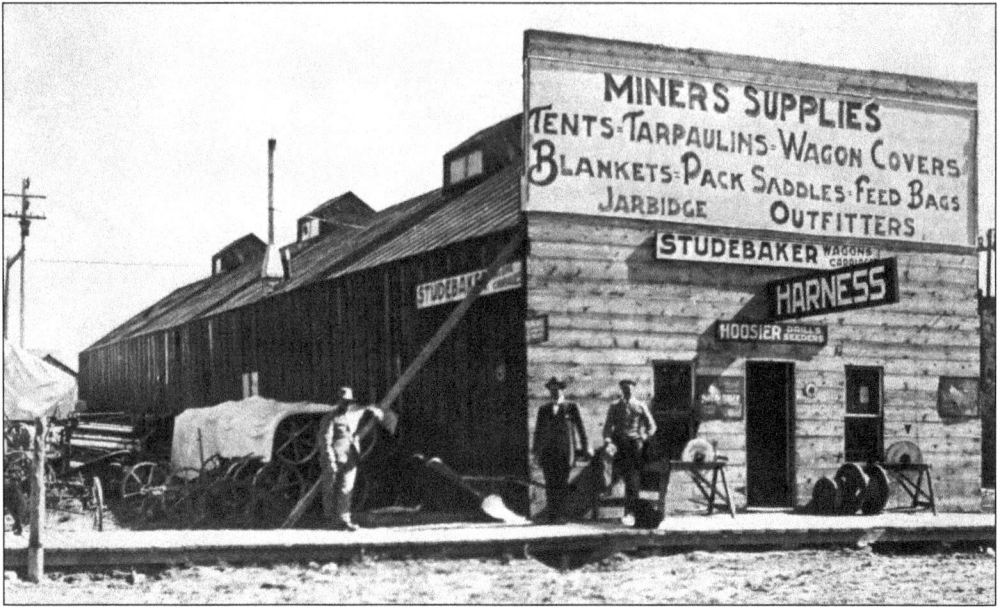

Mining activity in northern Nevada was another source of economic opportunity for Twin Falls and other towns on the tract, as their beginnings coincided with copper mining in Contact, which started in 1905, and gold mining in Jarbidge, which began in earnest in 1909. Businesses in Twin Falls and Buhl provided the last chance for prospectors to buy supplies before heading for the mining districts. The sign on the Buhl outfitting establishment indicates some of the supplies miners needed for their ventures in the isolated Nevada mountains. (Courtesy ISHS, 77-145.6.)

The tents in the photograph of Jarbidge illustrate the makeshift living conditions characteristic of mining camps. As early as 1911, residents had road access from the south and a telephone line, but production and jobs were sporadic and the availability of outside capital fluctuated wildly. Even so, mining activity in Jarbidge continued into the early 1930s, and copper was produced in Contact until the late 1950s.

Both Jarbidge and Contact were difficult to reach, and although a pack train or stage offered a long, dusty, and expensive option, routes from southern Idaho provided the easiest access. The rail line to Rogerson, built in 1910 to assist with the Salmon Falls Dam construction, shortened the trip.

The origins of the layout and early site planning of Twin Falls have their roots in the Louisiana Purchase Exposition, held in St. Louis in 1904. It was at this event that Clarence Hurtt, an officer in the Twin Falls Investment Company and Idaho's executive commissioner of the fair, most likely met the exposition's chief designer, Emmanuel Masqueray, a French-born architect who had worked with some of America's most prominent architects. Hurtt and Perrine, who also attended the fair, hired Masqueray to prepare the diagonal plan for the city, which John Hays

then surveyed. The siting of the park in the center of the town site is attributed to Masqueray. The county courthouse and the high school, built in classical styles, can be seen on the far side of the park in this photograph. Churches of a variety of faiths were built on streets bordering the park, and eventually the library was located opposite the courthouse. The result was a unified setting that provided a sense of urban grandeur on a small scale.

The Rogerson Hotel, seen in the foreground on the right, opened in December 1908 and provided both competition to the Perrine Hotel and anchored the south end of Twin Falls's commercial district. This photograph, probably taken in spring or summer 1909, shows how rapidly Twin Falls had developed since its founding five years earlier.

The owners of the Rogerson Hotel furnished it exclusively in Mission-style furniture, the popular style of the early 20th century. The photograph also indicates the light well that illuminated not only the lobby but also the individual 96 rooms.

Despite the hard work of starting their many ventures, Twin Falls citizens took time out to produce and enjoy plays and musical events. In February 1910, the Commercial and the Apollo clubs sponsored a production of Gilbert and Sullivan's *The Mikado*, which Bisbee noted was the city's first opera.

Perched on a base less than 5 square feet, Balanced Rock reportedly weighs over 40 tons and is almost five stories high. It is located about 5 miles west of Castleford, in the far western part of Twin Falls County.

Paving Twin Falls's streets in 1910 made a big difference in the comfort of its residents and in presenting the town as a modern city. Historian Jim Gentry notes that ethnic laborers constructed much of the city's infrastructure, and Greek and Italian laborers, employed by the Portland firm contracted for the street paving, were resented for taking jobs from unemployed residents.

Located at 150 Main Avenue South, the Twin Falls Hardware Company was an early and necessary business in Twin Falls. It supplied residents with not only the typical wares found in a hardware store but was also under contract with the Galligher Mining Company of Salt Lake to carry mining supplies for those bound for Jarbidge.

A parade of elephants presented an exotic sight through Twin Falls in 1910. They were heralding the arrival of the Hagenbeck-Wallace Circus, one of many traveling circuses in operation at the time. Circus parades also featured camels, lions, and tigers in cages and clowns.

William Jennings Bryan, who ran for president in 1896, 1900, and 1908, was a popular candidate in Idaho. He supported monetary policies advantageous to farmers but unfavorable to bankers and railroads. A gifted orator, he interrupted a two-week vacation in 1907 to speak to a local crowd from the steps of the Perrine Hotel. He and his family explored the area with their hosts, the Perrines, and his enthusiasm spilled over into a purchase of land on the Jerome town site.

The ornamental streetlights and the small trees in the Twin Falls City Park demonstrate the efforts city boosters went to establish amenities in their young community. The five-globe streetlights made of cast iron were a conscious attempt to create an urban landscape at an early date. The trees in the park were planted prior to the completion of the canal and ditch system in the town site and required watering by hand.

The dapper man in this photograph, proudly standing with his automobile, is situated in front of one of Twin Falls's earliest business, the Idaho Department Store. As its name implies, the store sold a variety of goods—clothes, groceries, and household items—and featured the "Economy Basement." Historian Leonard Arrington included his childhood trips to the "I. D." to purchase new school clothes as one his "lingering memories" of growing up in Twin Falls County.

Soldiers representing various military branches pose for a Bisbee photograph at the outset of World War I. Residents of the county rallied for their troops, establishing civil defense units, organizing a branch of the Red Cross, and raising over $3.5 million in Liberty Loans to support the war effort. Twenty-seven young men from Twin Falls County died in the Great War.

The railroad bridge under construction over Rock Creek Canyon seen in this photograph belies the anticipation of John Hayes when he surveyed the Twin Falls town site. He viewed Rock Creek Canyon as an amenity that would attract the nicest residential neighborhoods along its rim. The location of the train station near the canyon, however, ensured that industrial and warehouse uses would predominate in the western edge of the city.

Luxurious finishes, such as this marble in the Twin Falls National Bank, imparted a sense of permanence and stability to clients. The bank was organized in 1918, more than a decade after McCornick and Perrine established their banks. A publication from 1923 stated that the bank had the largest capital of any bank in the county, but it was the first bank failure in Twin Falls when it closed in 1931.

Built in 1905, this concrete block structure is one of Twin Falls's earliest buildings. F. W. Woolworth's occupied the building during the 1920s before it was converted into the Roxy Theater. The concrete block seen in this photograph was a popular material early in the 20th century for a variety of building types. Although the block was available commercially, individuals could also manufacture it once they purchased an inexpensive press and molding machine.

The dress and demeanor of the people in this photograph suggest that they were not earning their living through farming or manual labor. Census records of 1910 and city directories list a large number of Twin Falls residents employed as salespeople, clerks, and stenographers, indicating a sizable service economy.

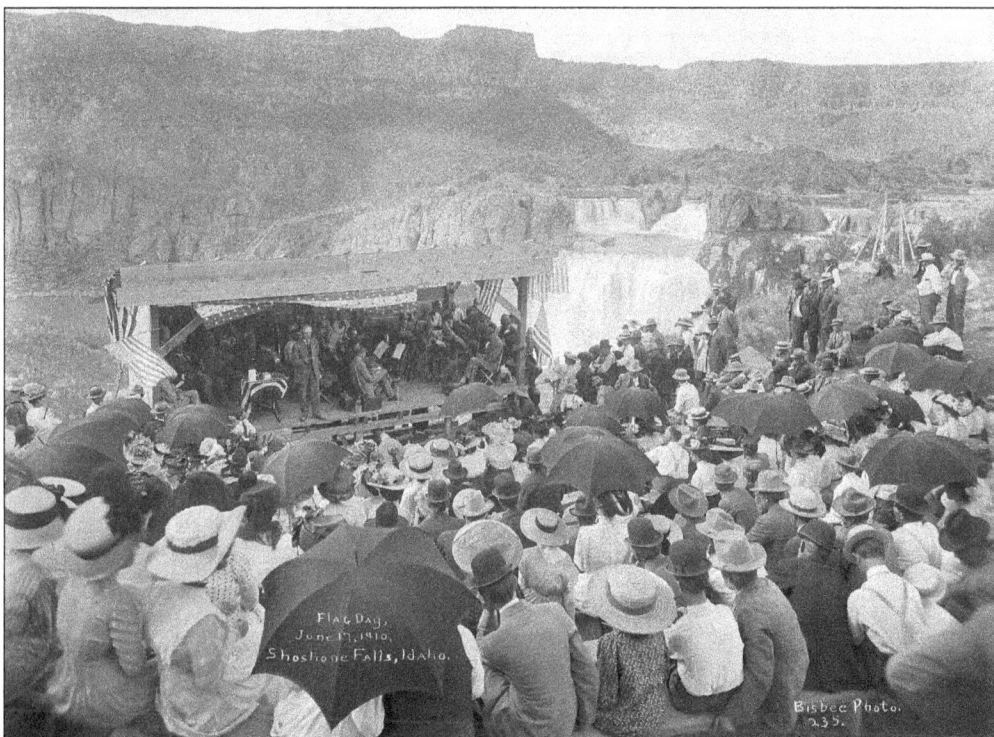

Crowds from both the north and south sides of the river turned out for Flag Day on June 17, 1910. Flags were raised on two points on either side of the canyon named for former presidents James Garfield and William McKinley. The organizers intended that the celebration would be an annual event to honor veterans and the flag, but 1912 was its last year. This Bisbee photograph provides a nice perspective of Shoshone Falls and Twin Falls in the distance.

Bisbee photographs indicate the transition of the Lind Auto Company from a utilitarian wood frame building to the owner's opulent terra cotta example seen in this image. Carl Lind started his business about 1908, selling Buicks and Cadillacs. Car dealers at that time sold not only automobiles but also gas and tires.

ENJOYING LIFE IN A BUICK.
BISBEE PHOTO-793.

Despite the rough roads and ever-present dust, automobiles offered an exciting way to explore the country. Adventurous drivers made headlines as they traveled from Boise to Salt Lake City or caravanned on the steep grades into the Snake River canyon. Here a small party enjoys the sight of Shoshone Falls; the eponymous hotel is seen in the background.

The Hansen Bridge, constructed in 1919 by the Midland Bridge Company of Kansas City, represented the first "rim-to-rim" crossing of the Snake River gorge. The bridge was a big improvement over taking the ferry or accessing the bridges that crossed the river at the bottom of the canyon. The two-lane bridge was suspended by 14 cables, measured just over 600 feet in length, and hovered almost 400 feet above the river. The bridge was replaced in 1966.

Born on a farm east of Twin Falls in 1917, Leonard Arrington was an esteemed western historian. He left for the University of Idaho with the intention of studying agriculture and returning to farming but turned instead to economics. After graduating from the University of Idaho, he earned a doctorate in economics from the University of North Carolina in 1952. His research and teaching elevated the scholarship of both Mormon history and the American West; his writing included both personal perspectives and expansive contexts. He died in 1999. (Courtesy LDS Church History Library.)

When the Twin Falls-Jerome Bridge opened in 1927, the bridge was 500 feet above the river and spanned a total of 1,350 feet across the canyon. Although the Hansen Bridge allowed people to cross the gorge without descending into the canyon, it was too far east for those travelling between Twin Falls and Jerome. On December 31, 1925, officials awarded the contract to construct the bridge to R. M. Murray, the construction engineer of the Hansen Bridge, who could then charge a toll to drivers and passengers. Murray designed a cantilever system, two Northwest firms constructed the bridge in 11 months, and they opened it on September 15, 1927, in time for the Jerome County Fair. Due to increased traffic, the bridge was replaced in the 1970s and renamed the Perrine Memorial Bridge.

Historians consider the Owsley Bridge, constructed in 1920, Idaho's most unique bridge. It represented a huge improvement for travelers over the Snake River between Twin Falls and Gooding counties, who previously relied on an inconvenient ferry crossing taking up to two hours. The water depth required a special design. In response, the nascent state public works department designed a cantilevered steel continuous through truss, the only one in Idaho. (Courtesy Dan Everhart, Idaho Department of Transportation.)

Seven

ESTABLISHING INSTITUTIONS

Most of the newcomers on the tract were U.S. citizens who desired to transplant the amenities and institutions they had left in their former communities. The establishment of schools, churches, and other public buildings underwent quick cycles of transition, as modern structures that could be seen in any established town quickly replaced temporary buildings.

At the same time, the settlement of Twin Falls County coincided with a national awareness for the importance of safety, sanitation, and comfort in both homes and institutional buildings. Up-to-date hospitals, libraries, and public safety facilities were considered essential not only for citizens' well being but also to attract economic growth. Reformers advocated for safer schools with plenty of ventilation, adequate fire egress, and good lighting.

Modern schools were built in Twin Falls and nearby towns, were constructed of brick, and were designed in specific styles. Rural schools, which were numerous in Twin Falls County, were of frame construction and consisted of two or three rooms that housed several grades per classroom. While the rural schools were not extravagant, they were spacious, comfortable, and offered a supportive learning environment to prepare students for high school.

As with schools, members of various religious denominations raised money and quickly erected church buildings. In Twin Falls, eight congregations had accepted the invitation to acquire lots from the investment company by April 1905. Denominations occasionally purchased each other's churches, depending on their needs and expansion plans. Due to the economic boom Twin Falls experienced in the 1910s, congregations enlarged or rebuilt their churches during that decade. Religious buildings in Twin Falls were built in a variety of contemporary styles, ranging from Gothic to Classical Revival styles.

Twin Falls County residents were enthusiastic about the construction of their most impressive civic structure, the county courthouse, located across the street from the city park. The county was established in 1907 and needed permanent quarters. When it opened in 1910, it was the tallest building in Twin Falls County and the only one to boast an elevator.

Named for Paul S. Bickel, the first mayor of Twin Falls and the chief engineer for the irrigation project, the Bickel School was constructed in 1906 and quickly overflowed with children. By November, 500 students were enrolled, including both elementary and high school grades. The school in this photograph was replaced by the existing Bickel School in 1938.

Because the Bickel School was bursting with students, voters approved a bond in 1908 to construct the Lincoln School north of downtown. The Boise firm of Wayland and Fennell designed the school in the Spanish Colonial Revival style. The parapets' scalloped edges, characteristic of this style, create a distinct silhouette seen in many early photographs.

School board members, public officials, and a large crowd attended a ceremony to lay the cornerstone of Lincoln School in July 1908. The Masons placed the stone, after marching from their hall a few blocks away. The event was so important that city businesses closed for the afternoon.

Constructed in 1909, the Central School in Filer illustrates the "central plan," in which classrooms were arranged on either side of a central stairwell. In the event of a fire, the stairwell acted as a flume that allowed the fire to quickly consume a building and provided no means of escape for students and teachers. Nationally, school officials abandoned the plan after tragic events and adopted a plan that located classrooms between two primary entrances.

The Buhl High School, completed in 1912, exemplifies a safer approach to school construction by providing stairwells at either end of the building. It also portrays the use of classical elements, with a heavy cornice, keystones above the arched windows, and a wide pediment over the classroom windows.

WASHINGTON SCHOOL.
BISBEE PHOTO-790.

Many Twin Falls residents remember the Washington School, demolished in 1975 and replaced with a strip mall. Its location at the intersection known as Five Points, the convergence of Shoshone Street, Blue Lakes Boulevard, and Addison Avenue, made it difficult for kids to cross so many streets. It opened in 1916 and differed from the other local schools in that it was only one story with a V-shaped plan.

Wayland and Fennell also designed the Twin Falls High School, this time in the neoclassical style. Its proximity to the county courthouse ensured that both buildings created an imposing presence on the north side of the park. The high school cost $150,000 to build and was constructed from 1910 to 1912. The size and design of the high school conveyed the message that Twin Falls was a progressive town. The building was demolished in 1979 to make way for a jail.

Young men labored over woodworking projects in a manual arts class at the Twin Falls High School, whereas young women learned cooking skills in the school's modern "electric kitchen." Educators at the turn of the 20th century pushed for the inclusion of shop, art, various crafts, and domestic science in the school curriculum. They debated whether such subjects should be taught for a future vocation or to reinforce learning in other subjects.

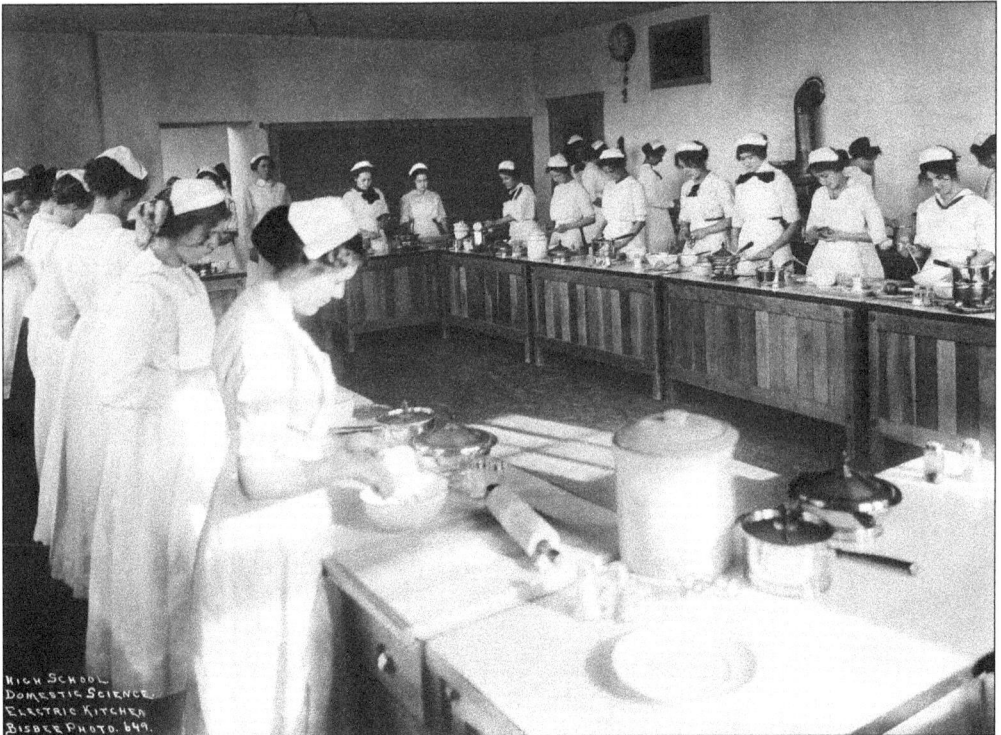

This photograph illustrates students diligently studying Latin. Large urban high schools in the early 20th century typically offered different tracks to students, allowing them to focus on business courses, manual training, or college preparatory subjects. Educational journals described schools with such options as "cosmopolitan," and the Twin Falls High School fell into this category.

The girls in this photograph are wearing modern workout clothes, around 1915, to exercise in the gymnasium of the Twin Falls High School.

High school auditoriums and gymnasiums also served as community gathering places used by a variety of organizations. The photograph above shows the spacious auditorium of the high school while not in use, while the image below shows the same space from the opposite perspective festooned for the fourth annual potato breakfast. The flowers on the tables are made from butter produced by a local dairy.

The Twin Falls Bruins had a winning season in 1935. They beat their arch rival Buhl, 20–0, and in fact, few of their opponents scored against them. Boise High School, however, beat Twin Falls in the state championship playoffs, 31–6.

These children are gathered in front of one of Twin Falls's earliest religious buildings, known as the Christian Church, located across the street from the city park near the library. In 1929, the building was sold to the Immanuel Lutheran Church, who enlarged the building 10 years later.

Constructed in 1910, the Pleasant Valley School was a two-room schoolhouse south of Kimberly. About 50 children attended during the 1920s and 1930s, with grades one through four taught in one room and grades five through eight in another. The school was the center of the Pleasant Valley community, which consisted of the farm families who lived in the area. Residents of Pleasant Valley enjoyed Christmas parties, box-lunch auctions, and picnics held at the school. After eighth grade, students attended high school in Kimberly. The school closed in 1947. This photograph dates to the 1970s, prior to its renovation as a private home. (Courtesy Twin Falls Public Library, G72.)

Everyone is wearing their best attire to attend church in the photograph above. The photograph below provides a full view of the elaborate massing of the building. The Presbyterians built this elaborate Gothic Revival church on Second Street North in the block west of the county courthouse, selling it to the Baptist congregation after 1916. This edifice was a temporary home for the Baptist church until they could raise the funds for a permanent home on Shoshone Street East.

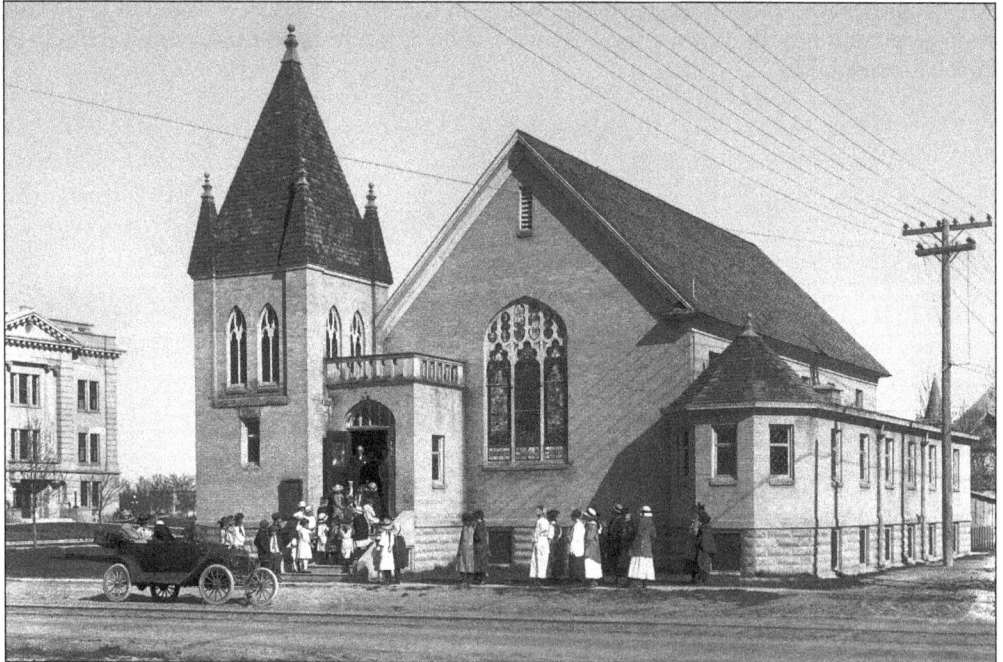

Methodists constructed the first phase of their church on the corner of Fourth Avenue East and Shoshone Avenue in 1909, seen in the photograph to the right. Bisbee recorded the laying of the cornerstone for the second phase of construction in 1917, seen below. Designed by B. Morgan Nisbet, the second phase featured brown sandstone, as opposed to the white brick used for the earlier structure, and was very different in style. Drawings of the church in both phases indicate the use of an "auditorium plan," popular in Protestant religions after the Civil War to emphasize the importance placed on oration, rather than ritual.

Contractor Pat Hall completed the small frame Catholic church in August 1905 (above). Hall was an early Twin Falls resident who constructed many buildings in the area. Parish members worshipped in this church for 16 years prior to the construction of St. Edward's (below), which was designed in the Renaissance Revival style by local architect Edward Gates. (Above, courtesy Twin Falls Public Library, G786; below, courtesy author.)

Begun in 1919 with volunteer labor, the Church of Jesus Christ of Latter-day Saints completed its tabernacle near the city park in January 1932. The postponement was attributed to high construction prices during the 1920s. When it was finished, the Classical Revival–style building was in keeping with the other imposing religious and civic institutions that surrounded the park. (Courtesy LDS Church History Library.)

Because adjoining lots were unavailable, the Ascension Episcopal Church declined a site fronting the park and instead chose to build on Third Avenue and Second Street North. The Rt. Rev. James A. Funston, Bishop of the Mission of Idaho, traveled to Philadelphia in 1907 to solicit donations to build this structure. It was completed in 1908, and a rectory was built the following year. (Courtesy Twin Falls Public Library, GB53.)

Twin Falls's first hospital was a vacated saloon in response to a typhoid epidemic in Rock Creek Canyon in 1905. Two years later, local organizers constructed a hospital at Third Avenue West and Third Street West, seen in the photograph above. After several remodels, it took on the look of the Georgian Revival–style building seen below. Although referred to as the Twin Falls Hospital, it was in fact privately owned by a Dr. Boyd. He protested strongly against the construction of a county-run institution that would compete with his facility. The county prevailed and built a new hospital and nurses' home on Addison Avenue West, just in time for the Spanish influenza epidemic in 1919. Dr. Boyd's hospital was converted into the Park Hotel.

Children pose in front of one of several makeshift libraries Twin Falls improvised before permanent quarters were constructed in 1939. Before occupying the McCollum building seen in this photograph, the library was housed in the second story of Frederick Harder's bakery, the courthouse, and the Idaho Light and Power Building on Main Street.

In 1906, when this photograph was taken, the Twin Falls fire department consisted of volunteers and operated out of a building donated by the town site company. The City of Twin Falls spent $220 for two hose carts. The station burned down at a later date and was rebuilt elsewhere. A paid department replaced the volunteer department in 1910.

117

The Twin Falls County Courthouse was one of 14 county courthouses built throughout Idaho between 1904 and 1922, reflecting the tripling of the state's population during those years. Twin Falls County was established in 1907 and was split off from Cassia County to the east. The architect, C. Harvey Smith, designed the courthouse in one of the classical variants popular for institutional buildings in the early 20th century. Here a crowd is gathered on Armistice Day.

Eight

The Comfort of Home

Domestic architecture in Twin Falls and surrounding towns followed a predictable trend: newcomers first built simple frame structures, easy to erect and inexpensive. If they prospered, they replaced the first house with a dwelling that was more spacious than their first home and more stylish. The area provided rich opportunity for people in the building trades, and the earliest city directories list plasterers, painters, carpenter, masons, and plumbers. Earl Felt, a builder, reported later in his life that he built 50 houses in Twin Falls in 1906 alone. Land developers saw no limits to the wealth they could reap, and early Twin Falls newspapers are filled with ads for new subdivisions. A promoter of the Graceland subdivision appealed to readers to "Get a Suburban Home and Raise Your Own Fruit, Garden and Chickens. It Will Make You Happy and Rich."

Obviously some homes were nicer than others, but a great disparity of income among residents was not apparent between homes in Twin Falls's neighborhoods and those of nearby towns. Although social class distinctions eventually solidified, for the first few years when everyone was new, an egalitarian spirit prevailed. Many households consisted of a traditional family and at least one boarder, often a teacher or a student. Boarding in a home was one alternative for those in a transitional phase of their lives; other options included living in a residential hotel, such as the Perrine Hotel or the Justamere Inn, renting a couple of rooms above retail uses in commercial buildings downtown, or renting a unit in the few available apartment buildings.

The opening of southern Idaho for development coincided with the popularity of the Craftsman bungalow. The optimism of the new community and the healthy climate of the region were especially well suited to the spirit of openness and outdoor living that the bungalow evoked. Bungalows also imparted a sense of comfort and shelter, important qualities to those living on an open, sagebrush plain. Nationally the popularity of the bungalow peaked in the late 1910s but hung on longer in the Twin Falls area. After the 1920s, the same styles in vogue elsewhere were used in southern Idaho.

The bungalows in these photographs can both be termed Craftsman in style. They display the common attributes associated with bungalows: wide eaves, broad porches, and exposed rafter ends and roof braces. The homes also illustrate how builders and owners created variety in the appearance of bungalows, such as changing the porch footprint, the dormer profile, and the combination of materials.

Hipped-roof dwellings like this one represent many of the earliest homes on the tract, although most were simpler without the complication of dormers, balconies, or porch railings. Usually they were of frame construction, had little embellishment, and their simple roof profile lent them to quick construction.

The living room of this bungalow exemplifies the Arts and Crafts aesthetic. This philosophy advocated the incorporation of handcrafted objects and building elements that emphasized, rather than obscured, natural materials. Here the owner adhered to these concepts by using quarter-sawn oak furniture, decorative ceramics, and rough-cut stone for the hearth.

The lack of a comfortable home did not keep this family and their guests from enjoying fresh watermelon on a hot summer day. The humble dwelling contrasts sharply with the Maxwell house (below), but in most instances homes in the area did not display such obvious income disparities.

John and Elizabeth Maxwell lived in this neoclassical-style home on Seventh Avenue East. It is no longer standing, but it was one of the most elaborate homes in Twin Falls. Maxwell was a cashier at the First National Bank, the financial institution founded by Perrine.

Architect Ed Gates and his family lived in this home in the teens on Tenth Avenue North, just a few homes away from another local architect, Burton Morse. Gates was one of the handful of architects in southern Idaho with formal training; in his case, he had studied at the University of Iowa. Gates's landmark building in Twin Falls is St. Edward's Catholic Church, completed in 1921.

George and Ruth Adams built this home in 1906 near the Bickel School. Adams was a partner in the Adams and Pilgerrim Lumber Company. The home is an excellent example of the Dutch Colonial Revival style, popular nationally from about 1905 to 1920. John and Millie Pilgerrim lived in the bungalow next door, built about the same time as the Adams's residence.

The house in this photograph is a perfect example of a type of house known as a Foursquare. Like the bungalow, it could be adapted to a variety of styles and also presented an appearance of homeyness and comfort. In Twin Falls County, it was used more frequently for farmhouses, but many examples can be found in Twin Falls and in neighboring towns.

This photograph, taken early in Twin Falls's development, illustrates the layout of the neighborhoods of the original town site. These residential areas are still characterized by modest outbuildings at the rear of lots, accessed by alleys.

The Justamere Inn, as with other local hotels, served not only a clientele needing rooms for a few nights but also long-term boarders. Known as "residence hotels," they provided an alternative to rooming houses or boarding with a family for those in a transitional phase of their lives. The Justamere Inn was built near the courthouse in 1910. The Lincoln School is visible in the background.

Mark and Elizabeth Murtaugh's residence on Blue Lakes Boulevard was one of many handsome homes that made the street an impressive entryway into Twin Falls. A civil engineer, Murtaugh was the assistant manager of the Twin Falls Water and Canal Company. He left Idaho about 1905 to work in Brazil and returned to Twin Falls in 1907.

The H.S. BOLTON HOME 9/1/09
BISBEE 140

These Bisbee photographs provide an interesting look at a country home under construction and the outcome. The small barn on the right of the house was more typical of outbuildings in the area than the large structure built for the Kunze dairy operation seen earlier. Basalt, seen in the foundation in the above photograph, was used for foundations and walls that would be on less visible parts of a building. This Dutch colonial house was built for S. H. Bolton.

Home of S. H. Bolton.
Built June 1908.
Trees planted 1909.
10 A. Tract joining Twin Falls City.

Bisbee Photo. 141
1910.

Visit us at
arcadiapublishing.com

www.ingramcontent.com/pod-product-compliance
Lightning Source LLC
Chambersburg PA
CBHW050604110426
42813CB00008B/2455